THE STORY OF SPACE

SPACE STATIONS

Steve Parker

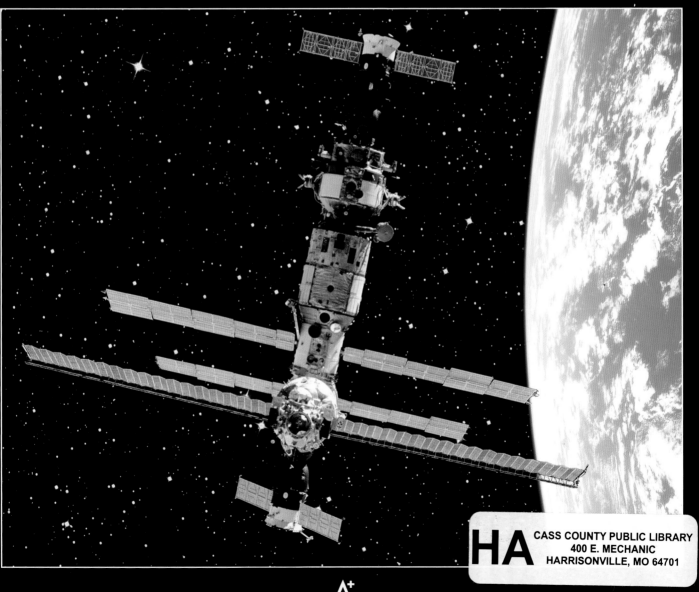

A⁺
Smart Apple Media

Published by Smart Apple Media, an imprint of Black Rabbit Books
P.O. Box 3263, Mankato, Minnesota 56002
www.blackrabbitbooks.com

Produced by David West ☼☼ Children's Books
6 Princeton Court, 55 Felsham Road, London SW15 1AZ

Designed by Gary Jeffrey

Cataloging-in-Publication Data is available from the Library of Congress.
ISBN 978-1-62588-081-9

CSPIA compliance information: DWCB14FCP
011014

9 8 7 6 5 4 3 2 1

All images courtesy of NASA except: p12t, de Benutzer HPH; p24tr, NASA/Bill Ingalls; p27b,
NASA/Tracy Caldwell Dyson; p29b, J.Simmons

CONTENTS

Roughly the size of a football field, the International Space Station (ISS) is by far the largest human-made structure placed into orbit. Most of its parts were delivered by the now-retired Shuttle fleet. The ISS is a triumph of space engineering and a model of international cooperation.

INTRODUCTION

Since the first space station launched in 1971, human presence in orbit has been almost constant. Yet living in space poses massive challenges in technology, biology, and funding. How do we build in orbit? How are astronauts provided with life support and protected from extremes of heat and cold, microgravity, and radiation? Solving these problems costs vast sums and tests our ingenuity. But our orbital foothold is precious—for science and spaceflight, and as an inspiring human achievement.

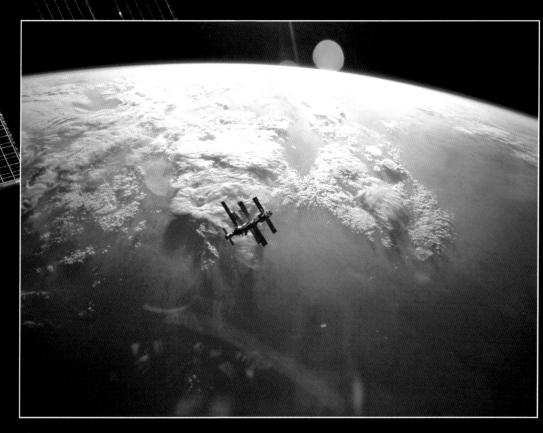

The Russian space station Mir circled the planet in Low Earth Orbit, LEO. Space stations are typically placed here, below an altitude of 300 miles (482 km). LEO is near enough for ferry craft to reach, but high enough to minimize atmospheric drag.

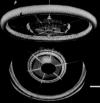

SPACE COLONIES

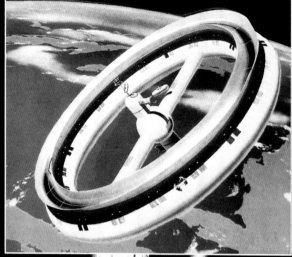

From the 1950s to the early 1970s, ideas for space stations stimulated the imagination of scientists and space planners. They envisioned giant space wheels and even "cities in the skies."

WHEEL LIFE

The 1975 *Stanford Torus* design was a donut-shaped ring 1 mile (1.6 km) in diameter, which rotated once every minute to provide Earth-like gravity. Sunlight was controlled by a giant mirror placed at an angle to the ring, which housed 10,000 people and had agricultural areas for growing crops.

The *Torus* concept came from a question posed by Princeton physicist Gerard K. O'Neill: "Is the surface of a planet really the right place for an expanding technological civilization?" Calculations showed it was more economical to build self-sustaining space colonies, mine the Moon and asteroids for raw materials, and harness the incredible power of the Sun out in space.

This imaginary scene shows astronauts fitting the final pieces of radiation shielding to the outer ring of a Stanford Torus. The station would lie at a gravitational balance point between Earth and the Moon, to avoid the need for orbit-adjusting engines.

The power and cost of Earth-launched rockets limits the size of objects put into space. A mass driver (electric catapult) on the Moon, which has one-sixth of Earth's gravity, could launch parts made there more economically.

SPHERES OF INFLUENCE

Like the *Torus*, a *Bernal Sphere* works like a planet turned inside out. Everything is built on an axis that rotates, producing centrifugal force to simulate gravity. At the end of each axis are low-gravity manufacturing plants and docking ports. The outside of the habitation sphere is built from lunar waste slag (to shield radiation), then "terraformed" with a river running through the middle, its beaches made of softened lunar sand.

The Bernal Sphere's crops and livestock lie in a separate compartmentalized torus, where lower gravity and unfiltered sunlight aid plant growth.

The **Space Colony DREAMERS** were **inspired** by **APOLLO** to **see** the **MOON** as a future **RESOURCE**

BERNAL SPHERE

1. **DOCKING PORT**
2. **RADIATORS** Remove excess heat
3. **EXTERNAL AGRICULTURAL TORUS**
4. **FACTORIES** In a microgravity environment
5. **MIRRORS** To reflect sunlight into the habitation sphere. Arrays of solar panels (not shown) provide electricity
6. **SHIELDED HABITAT** Land space for 10,000 humans

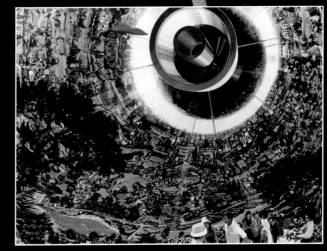

The center of the habitation sphere would house a low-gravity recreation area for "zero-gee" sports and human-powered flight.

SKYLAB

The US's first space station was a budget version built of left-over parts from canceled Moon missions. Despite many early problems, *Skylab* proved a durable space laboratory and home for 171 days.

In July 1973, an Apollo spacecraft carried the second crew of Skylab (SL-3) to the station, 146 miles (235 km) above Earth. The first crew had already departed.

SKYLAB

1. **ORBITAL WORKSHOP**
2. **AIRLOCK MODULE**
3. **MULTIPLE DOCKING ADAPTER** MDA
4. **APOLLO TELESCOPE MOUNT** Solar observatory
5. **SUN SHIELD** Emergency structure

SKYLAB SPACE STATION

Solar array

1

5

2

4

3

Hatch

APOLLO COMMAND/ SERVICE MODULE

Solar array

PRECARIOUS BEGINNINGS

Skylab was built inside an empty Saturn S-IVB third-stage rocket. It carried a solar observatory adapted from an Apollo Lunar Module descent stage. The station was launched unmanned on May 14, 1973. But at high altitude, the thin atmosphere ripped away its micrometeoroid sun shield, trashing one solar panel and jamming the other.

In orbit, *Skylab* was forced to run on low power and began to overheat. On May 23 the first three-man launch, SL-2, became a rescue mission as the crew deployed a hastily made sun shield and released the jammed solar array.

The launch mission Skylab 1 (SL-1) was the last lift-off for the mighty Saturn V moon rocket.

Mission patch for Skylab 4 (the misnumbering of 3 was a NASA error).

SKYLAB 3
CARR-GIBSON-POGUE

"On duty, the most fun was looking out the window."
Gerald Carr, Skylab 4 commander

SKY LIFE

Skylab comprised a large laboratory or workspace with a smaller living area beneath and waste tanks behind. After making the station habitable, the first crew spent 28 days performing microgravity and medical experiments, and recording the Sun's activities. They departed on June 22.

Crew SL-3 arrived on July 28 for an extended 59-day mission. The final crew, SL-4, docked on November 16. They had to contend with gyroscope problems and space sickness, yet they managed a record 84-day stay. NASA hoped its Space Shuttles would reactivate *Skylab* in the 1980s. It was not to be.

A view from the docking adapter (below) shows the main workshop with living area below. On such long flights, hygiene was important. Bathing in the sealed vacuum chamber is demonstrated by Jack Lousma of SL-3 (right).

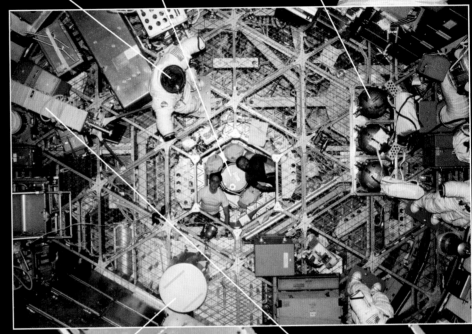

EVA suit   Waste hatch   Nitrogen propellant

Astronaut weighing machine

Waste odor filter

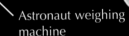

Owen Garriot of SL-3 helped fit an extra sunshade to the station. Garriot found EVA (Extra Vehicular Activity) personally thrilling: "Like looking down this very long elevator shaft to Earth."

Increased **SOLAR ACTIVITY thickened** Earth's outer **ATMOSPHERE**, bringing *SKYLAB* down **three years** early on **JULY 11, 1979.**

SALYUT

SALYUT 1

While the US aimed for the Moon, the USSR (Soviet Union) launched the world's first purpose-designed space station, *Salyut 1,* on April 19, 1971. Its mission was beset with frustration and tragedy.

SOYUZ 11

The Salyut 1 *station was based on* Almaz, *a simple two-cylinder military design fitted with a docking adapter for Soyuz spacecraft.*

SALYUT 6

1. **LABORATORY COMPARTMENT**
2. **COMMAND SECTION**
3. **TRANSFER COMPARTMENT** To EVA and Soyuz airlocks
4. **DOCKING HATCH**
5. **SOLAR ARRAY**
6. **RCS THRUSTERS** Attitude control

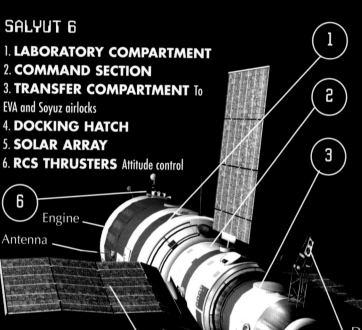

Engine
Antenna
6
5
Porthole
Docking radar
1
2
3
4

DEATH IN SPACE

On April 23, *Soyuz 10* lifted off with a three-man crew bound for *Salyut 1.* But they were unable to dock successfully and so had to abort their mission.

On June 7, *Soyuz 11* reached the station and the crew managed to occupy it for 23 days—until a minor fire forced them home. As their capsule separated from its service module on reentry, it was damaged and lost its air. All three astronauts suffocated and died.

LATER SALYUTS

The accident temporarily grounded all Soyuz spacecraft and *Salyut 1* fell to Earth in October 1971. Two years later *Salyut 2,* an adapted *Almaz* spy station, failed to orbit. At last in 1975 *Salyut 4* set crew endurance records of 30 and 63 days, until the environmental system broke down, rendering the station damp and moldy. But the Soviets were learning. *Salyuts 6* and *7* were first to have docks at both ends, meaning crews could stay on board as unmanned ferry craft brought supplies. *Salyut 6* hosted stays of six months. From 1982, *Salyut 7* was crewed three times—longest stay 237 days. In 1985, unoccupied, it mysteriously went dead.

Damaged Salyut 7 *spins crazily.*

Svetlana Savitskaya, part of the Soyuz T-7 crew, became the first woman to spacewalk on July 25, 1984, while aboard Salyut 7.

Vladimir Dzhanibekov

Viktor Savinykh

SAVING SALYUT 7

An electrical fault had drained *Salyut 7*'s batteries. But the station, equipped with advanced environmental, power, and navigation systems, was too valuable to lose. On June 6, 1985, Vladimir Dzhanibekov and Viktor Savinykh of the *Soyuz T-13* crew reached the inert, rolling station. Dzhanibekov used their own Soyuz thrusters to match the station's rotation for docking. They opened the hatch and floated through. The station's air was icy cold but breathable. Frost coated the walls.

The astronauts isolated the fault and used their *Soyuz* to re-angle the station's solar arrays and recharge its batteries. Carefully, system by system, *Salyut 7* was brought back online.

The crew having restored power with a landmark orbit repair, Soyuz T-13 drifts away from Salyut 7. The station would later see the first orbital handover between two station crews.

The **Salyut DESIGN** would **form** the **BASIS** of **CORE RUSSIAN** modules in the future *MIR* and *ISS*.

GOING MODULAR

The Salyut series paved the way for *Mir* ("Peace" or "Community"), a modular design built from sections assembled in orbit. *Mir* was also the first space station to be permanently occupied.

Mir began with a core module based on the venerable Salyuts. A six-port docking node allowed extra modules to be attached in space, and if necessary, even moved around.

PROGRESS CARGO SHIP

KVANT 1

Docking node

CORE MODULE

A new automated Soyuz spacecraft called Progress delivered supplies for each six-month Mir mission. Crew changeovers were handled by the Soyuz TM, a stronger, lighter, advanced version of this tried-and-tested spacecraft.

SOYUZ TM SPACECRAFT

CORE VALUES

The core module of *Mir* was launched on February 19, 1986, atop a Proton heavy-lift rocket, to a height of 214 miles (344 km). Unlike *Salyut*, the core module was empty of instruments; but it did have two berths ready to receive the set-up crew, T-15, on March 15.

The first module attached was Kvant 1, arriving on April 12, 1987, hauled by a robotic space tug. Kvant 1 was an astrophysics laboratory equipped with X-ray and ultraviolet telescopes and also six gyrodynes—electrically driven wheels spinning at 10,000 rpm—to take over attitude (positional) control from the core's rockets.

The main window of Mir's core module had a tiny crew cabin window above.

The core module was designed as a living area housing bunks, medical equipment, and a command center with Earth link. Later in the mission, excercise machines were bolted to the floor.

"Mir *is an outpost, a presence on the frontier that is kept at a cost that exceeds its real or potential material return.*"

Frank Culbertson, NASA, Shuttle-Mir

MIR SPACE STATION

1. **CORE MODULE** Central control and habitation, began orbiting 1986
2. **KVANT 1** Astronomy, docked 1987
3. **KVANT 2** Utility unit with new life-support system, docked 1989
4. **KRISTALL** Microgravity materials science, geophysics, astrophysics, docked 1990
5. **DOCKING MODULE** Space Shuttle compatible docking port, docked 1995
6. **SPEKTR** Shuttle/MIR experiments, US crew quarters, docked 1995
7. **PIRODA** Remote sensing module, synthetic aperture radar dish, docked 1996

Mir's docking node hatches led to other modules or docked spacecraft.

STATION ASSEMBLY

Each of the next four modules was based on the military TKS spacecraft, a large ferry originally designed to service *Almaz* space stations. The first, Kvant 2, arrived in orbit in November 1989. It was a utility module bringing the Elektron oxygen generator, water recycling and regeneration, an airlock—and a crew shower.

Kvant 2 fired its engines to chase the station. On catching up, it docked first with the front port on the node and extended its Lyappa mechanical arm to fix onto the node. Then the arm raised and rotated Kvant 2 to its final position on a side port. The following Kristall, Spektr, and Piroda modules all docked in a similar way.

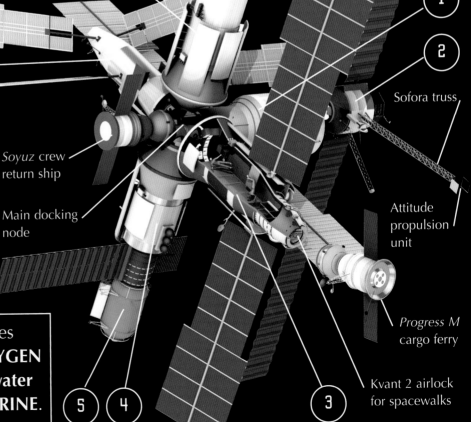

Solar arrays

Soyuz crew return ship

Main docking node

Sofora truss

Attitude propulsion unit

Progress M cargo ferry

Kvant 2 airlock for spacewalks

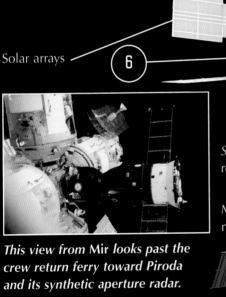

This view from Mir looks past the crew return ferry toward Piroda and its synthetic aperture radar.

ELEKTRON life **support** uses **electricity** to **separate OXYGEN** from **WATER**—including **water** purified from the **crew's URINE.**

MIR: MISSIONS

At the end of 1991, the Soviet Union as a nation fell apart. High above, *Mir* drifted in limbo, two modules still to be fitted. Its crew were dubbed "the last Soviet citizens."

KVANT 1

Sofora girder

CORE MODULE

Space Shuttle Atlantis joined with Mir in June 1985, forming the largest space structure at the time.

Docking node

SPEKTR

VDU thruster block

KRISTALL (moved on the docking node so the Shuttle could clear the solar arrays, see opposite)

KVANT 2

Buran docking adapter

FINANCIAL RESCUE

RSA, the Russian Space Agency, agreed to a program of US cooperation in exchange for NASA funding of *Mir*. The Spektr module was finally launched with equipment and habitation for US astronauts and Shuttle *Atlantis* was fitted with a docking adapter for *Mir*. In the meantime, US President Bill Clinton agreed with Russian President Boris Yeltsin that the two countries would

SHUTTLE ORBITER *ATLANTIS*

Orbiter Docking System (ODS)

Routine maintenance on Mir's unpressurized sections meant numerous spacewalks.

be partners in a future International Space Station, the *ISS*. The Shuttle-*Mir* missions acted as a training ground for the next generation of station-builders and spacefarers.

This replacement gyrodyne was carried by a Shuttle to Mir.

Mir's international crews dined together in the core module, giving them the chance to try out each other's space food.

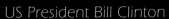

ORBITAL ENDURANCE

On Shuttle-*Mir*, space exploration changed from competition to cooperation. The Russians had the most experience with long-duration flights, since Shuttle missions were limited to two weeks. RSA and NASA astronauts performed dual spacewalks in their respective spacesuits. They trained in each other's languages and tested each other's methods.

In April 1996 the delivery of Piroda, an Earth survey module, completed *Mir*. Overall, Shuttles visited *Mir* 11 times, exchanging crews and bringing supplies and equipment.

Shannon Lucid floats through the Spektr module during her record American long-duration spaceflight of 188 days.

SEVEN NASA **astronauts** had **RESIDENCIES** on *MIR* for a **total STAY TIME** of **975 DAYS**.

Soyuz TM

KVANT 2

A Russian-made, US-funded dual docking module arrived in November 1995. This meant Kristall could stay on its original port during future Shuttle visits—a far safer arrangement (see opposite).

SPEKTR

Core module

KRISTALL

Shuttle remote-operated Canadarm

Original docking node

Dual docking module

Shuttle cargo bay

Orbiter Docking System (ODS)

FIRE IN SPACE

Jerry Linenger, the fourth US astronaut to visit *Mir*, began his stay on January 12, 1997. He took part in several "firsts"— first NASA crew member to spacewalk in a Russian suit, first Shuttle crew to undock in a Soyuz, and first to see a big accident on *Mir*...

Juggling balls: life in microgravity could be a lot of fun.

EMERGENCY!

On February 23, 1997, *Mir* was crowded. Arriving Russians Tsibkiev and Lazutkin had brought a German visitor, Ewald, who would return with the two leaving astronauts Korzun and Kaleri. Solid-fuel oxygen generators (SFOGs) were running to improve air quality.

In Kvant, Lazutkin switched on another SFOG—which erupted in flames! Korzun barreled into the hatchway to pull him clear. A fire extinguisher failed, toxic smoke filled the station, and the crew donned respirators as the fire raged.

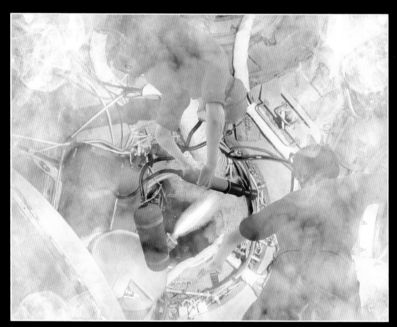

Oxygen respirators protected the crew while the SFOG burned "like a blowtorch." Collecting fire extinguishers from all over the station, the crew worked in pairs until the blaze was out.

Linenger and the others wore respirators for several hours as Mir's air circulation filters gradually cleansed the station of smoke.

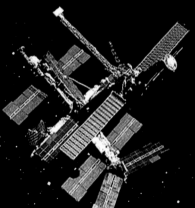

At one stage on Linenger's mission, the station suffered a loss of attitude control. It caused an alarming, slow, uncontrolled "tumble" through space.

Linenger's replacement, Michael Foale, witnessed an accident on June 25, 1997...

PROGRESS

...while testing a new Progress ferry docking system. Vasily Tsibliyev lost control of the ferry and crashed it into Spektr, damaging solar panels (below) and causing a slow leak. Spektr was sealed off and Mir lost much power.

After the Spektr accident, later in 1997 crews spacewalked inside it. They rerouted power cables and new controls for the solar arrays. This restored two-thirds of Mir's original power.

END OF MIR

June 8, 1998: Space Shuttle *Discovery* undocked from *Mir*, ending their joint missions—since NASA wanted to focus its finds on the upcoming *ISS*. RSA announced that *Mir* would be deorbited in 1999. Meanwhile, life on the station continued with visits by many "guest" astronauts. RSC Energia, the company that now owned *Mir*, called for private funding. MirCorp was formed and a manned service and repair mission took place—but the real money never appeared. In March 2001, a *Progress* ferry intentionally dipped *Mir* into the atmosphere and a spectacular fiery end over the Pacific.

ENGINEERED to last **FIVE** years, *MIR* was **kept going** for **15**.

Battered by accidents, worn out, and dirty, the $4.2 billion station that was Mir sank toward the end of its life in 2001.

A JOINT EFFORT

The 1990s saw the start of a new space station—a mix of parts from Russia's planned *Mir 2* and the US's *Freedom*. Both were 1980s concepts that never left the drawing board. Now, their time had come.

NASA Shuttle Orbiter
Endeavour

ORBITAL UNION

The first piece of the unnamed station would be a power, communication, and spaceflight module—the Functional Cargo Block (FCB) named Zarya. This was an all-Russian design based on the TKS ferry, paid for by NASA, and built over two years by Boeing and the RSA in Russia. On November 20, 1998, it launched and automatically unfurled its solar wings above Earth before boosting to a 240-mile (386-km) orbit.

On December 4, Shuttle *Endeavour* delivered Unity, a US-designed and built connecting node. After three spacewalks, Unity and the FCB were linked. Unity's six docking ports could now receive the US's parts of the station.

Endeavour left Unity and Zarya joined and functional. Until new modules arrived, Zarya controlled the station's position using its 36 steering jets.

Endeavour's STS-88 crew tested one of the Pressurized Mating Adapters (PMAs). These were heated docking tunnels between modules and also to visiting spacecraft.

PMA 1

ZARYA (RUSSIAN FCB, FUNCTIONAL CARGO BLOCK)

UNITY (AMERICAN CONNECTING NODE ONE)

PMA 2 TUNNEL LINK

ZARYA has a **DESIGN life** of **15 YEARS** but may **EXCEED** that by **another 10 YEARS.**

> *"To me, the biggest challenge is trying to pack 30 hours into an 18-hour work day."* — *Expedition 1* commander William Shepherd

A Proton heavy-lift rocket carried Russian service module Zvezda ("Star") into orbit. Proton featured a clustered six-engine first stage, three second-stage engines, and single-engine third stage. It raised into Low Earth Orbit up to 21 tons (19 t)—about 40% of the US Saturn V's load.

On July 2000, Zarya and Unity were remotely guided and docked with Zvezda. Featuring a four-port node, lab, and living quarters, Zvezda became the core of the Russian section of the station.

Docking node

Solar arrays

ZVEZDA SERVICE MODULE

Unpressurized antennae, propellant, and thruster assembly

FITTING OUT

After four more Shuttle visits, the station was ready for permanent occupation. Hardware, from batteries and computers to excercise machines, was installed.

In October 2000 the Z1 truss was fitted to Zvezda—the first component of the station's "backbone."

Progress refueling ship

Shuttle crews spacewalked to install the first truss frame) and a third PMA link. Water and food were stowed.

The first long-stayers, *Expedition 1*, arrived on a Soyuz flight on October 31, 2000. They opened the hatch to Zvezda and cool clean air; the preceding Shuttle crew, STS-92, had activated life support. But Unity remained in shutdown until larger solar arrays were delivered. *Expedition 1* got busy setting up communications, unloading ferry craft, and preparing to expand the still-unnamed station.

Among Expedition 1, the lack of a station name bothered ex-navy Commander Shepherd. On the first radio link he requested the station be called Alpha—at least during his stay.

William Shepherd

Sergei K. Krikalev

Yuri Gidzenko

BUILDING THE ISS

Early missions to the new orbital home—the *International Space Station, ISS,* as it became known—focused on expanding the structure with lab, airlocks, and trusses.

ALL TRUSSED UP

The *ISS*'s Integrated Truss Structure (ITS) is an American innovation carried over from the original Space Station *Freedom* design. The ITS supports unpressurized equipment carriers,

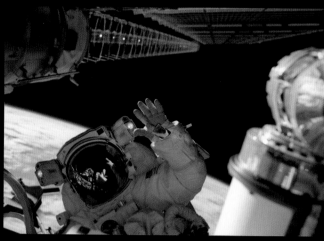

The first US-made Solar Array Wings (SAWs) were installed on STS-97, allowing Unity to be powered up.

radiators (to remove heat from the massed electronics inside the station), and solar arrays. The first segment of the ITS, the P6 (sixth port, or left-hand) truss was fitted to the Z1 (first zenith, or upward) truss for temporary solar arrays.

On February 9, 2001, the US Destiny lab unit arrived on board STS-98 . The first experiments were brought by **Expedition 2.**

In March 19, 2001, *Expedition 1* finally went home via Shuttle. *Expedition 2* brought the first experiments aboard—racks of laboratory equipment designed to fit inside Destiny's bays. Shuttle flights brought the first External Stowage Platform, to stow spare parts—and the all-important Canadarm 2 robotic arm.

The Quest Joint Airlock, fitted in August 2001, is the ISS's main spacewalk portal. It houses spacesuits and other facilities for astronauts going outside.

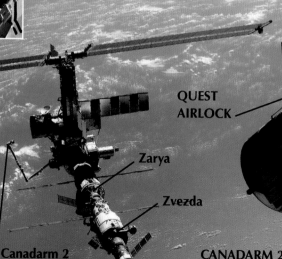

Shown here in April 2002, the ISS boasts Canadarm 2, also called the Space Station Remote Manipulator System (SSRMS). Fitted during STS-100, it plays key roles in building and maintenance.

QUEST AIRLOCK

Zarya

Zvezda

Canadarm 2

CANADARM 2

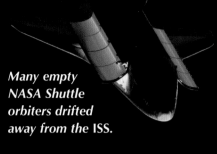

Many empty NASA Shuttle orbiters drifted away from the ISS.

In September 2001 a modified Progress ferry brought PIRS, a docking/airlock module. It allowed astronauts to spacewalk in their Orlan suits from the Earth-facing side, or nadir, of Zvezda.

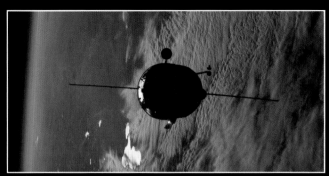

POINTS AND RAILROADS

Canadarm 2 is self-locatable, moving inchworm-like between Power Data Grapple Fixtures (PDGFs) at various points on the station. With the addition of the S0 truss and the Mobile Base System (MBS), it gained a trackway with a powered cart eventually running the whole length of the truss. The cart can also carry spacewalking astronauts and equipment. Two more big trusses, P1 (Port = left) and S1 (Starboard = right), were added before the Shuttle fleet was grounded in 2003 due to the *Columbia* tragedy.

A Soyuz lifeboat waits in a parking orbit to rejoin the station.

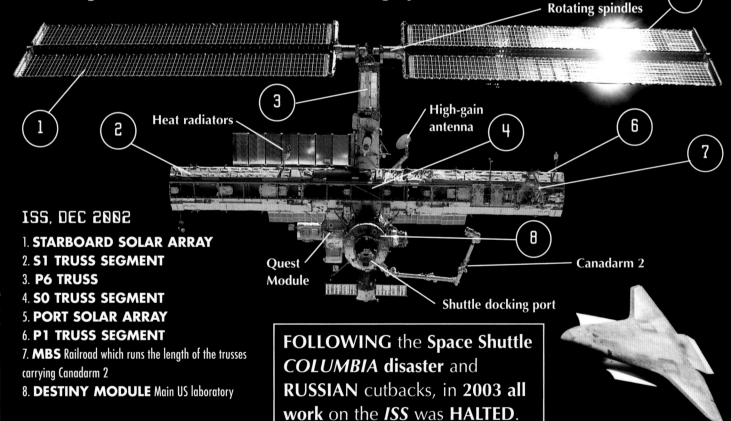

Rotating spindles

Heat radiators

High-gain antenna

Quest Module

Shuttle docking port

Canadarm 2

ISS, DEC 2002

1. **STARBOARD SOLAR ARRAY**
2. **S1 TRUSS SEGMENT**
3. **P6 TRUSS**
4. **S0 TRUSS SEGMENT**
5. **PORT SOLAR ARRAY**
6. **P1 TRUSS SEGMENT**
7. **MBS** Railroad which runs the length of the trusses carrying Canadarm 2
8. **DESTINY MODULE** Main US laboratory

FOLLOWING the **Space Shuttle** *COLUMBIA* **disaster** and **RUSSIAN** cutbacks, in **2003 all work** on the *ISS* was **HALTED**.

COMPLETING THE ISS

From 2003 the *ISS* had only two crew, to keep it semi-active. In 2006 NASA agreed to 17 more Shuttle flights to finish construction before the planes retired.

THE INTERNATIONALS

A series of six Shuttle missions delivered the *ISS*'s last big truss sections, solar arrays, and expanded science facilities. The European Space Agency (ESA) Columbus module was connected to Harmony's starboard berthing socket, and on the port socket, the Japanese Experimental Module (JEM).

JEM is made up of a pressurized lab, an unpressurized storage module, and a platform with equipment exposed to space and positioned by a robot arm. It is operated by the Japanese space agency, JAXA. In 2009 the Russians attached Poisk, a second docking/airlock module, to Zvezda.

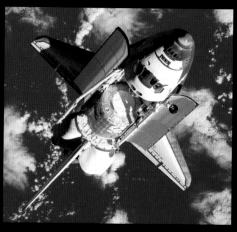

Discovery arrived in 2007 with node 2, Harmony. The final part of the US core, Harmony increased living space and provided six expansion points.

On its last ever mission in 2011, Endeavour scanned its own heat shield for problems — a routine safety check after Columbia's destruction.

Orbital Boom Sensor system

Columbus

ATV

JEM

Harmony

P3/P4 truss

Astronaut Hans Schlegel prepares the ESA lab Columbus for use by the German Aerospace Center (DLR).

Canadian robot helper Dextre arrived in 2008. It can be fixed to grapple fixtures or Canadarm 2.

Dextre

P6 truss

ESA Automated Transfer Vehicles (ATVs) — unmanned supply ships — began service in 2008. After unloading, they are filled with waste and destroyed during reentry.

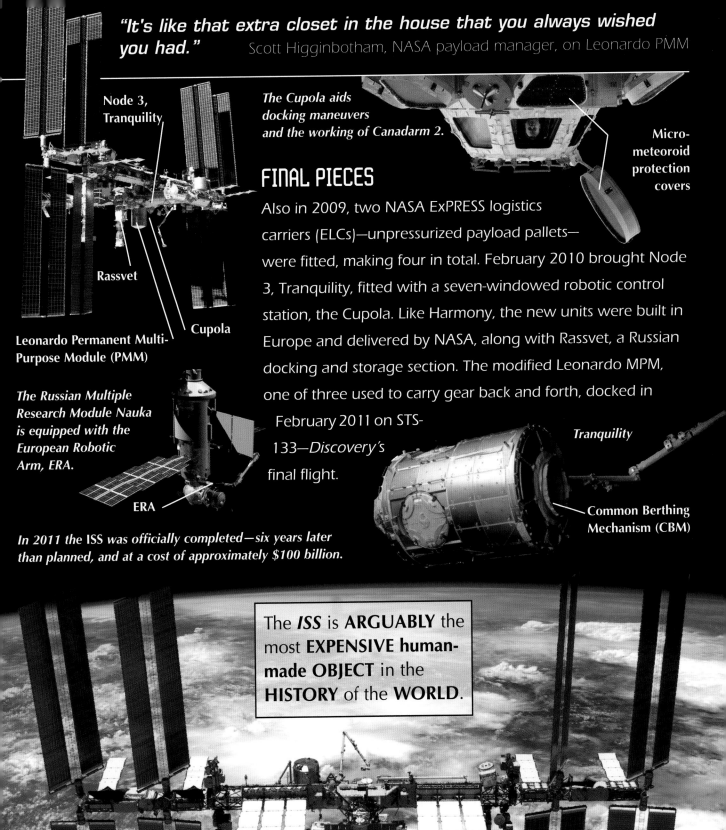

Node 3, Tranquility

The Cupola aids docking maneuvers and the working of Canadarm 2.

Micro-meteoroid protection covers

FINAL PIECES

Also in 2009, two NASA ExPRESS logistics carriers (ELCs)—unpressurized payload pallets— were fitted, making four in total. February 2010 brought Node 3, Tranquility, fitted with a seven-windowed robotic control station, the Cupola. Like Harmony, the new units were built in Europe and delivered by NASA, along with Rassvet, a Russian docking and storage section. The modified Leonardo MPM, one of three used to carry gear back and forth, docked in February 2011 on STS-133—*Discovery's* final flight.

Rassvet

Cupola

Leonardo Permanent Multi-Purpose Module (PMM)

The Russian Multiple Research Module Nauka is equipped with the European Robotic Arm, ERA.

ERA

In 2011 the ISS was officially completed—six years later than planned, and at a cost of approximately $100 billion.

Tranquility

Common Berthing Mechanism (CBM)

The *ISS* is **ARGUABLY** the most **EXPENSIVE human-made OBJECT** in the **HISTORY** of the **WORLD**.

ISS EXPEDITIONS

Missions to the *ISS* are called expeditions and are made up of a commander and five flight engineers. Each expedition is a combination of station management and science.

Expeditions begin with the launch of a Soyuz TMA rocket at Baikonur Cosmodrome in Kazakhstan, carrying three of the crew.

SPACE RESIDENCY

The *ISS* is maintained and run by five national space agencies: NASA, Russia's Roscosmos, ESA, JAXA, and the Canadian Space Agency (CSA). The station is a platform for biology, astrophysics, and space hardware experiments in continuous microgravity. The human-run laboratories are far more flexible than unmanned satellites doing similar work in orbit.

Sections of the ISS are flight-controlled by their host space agencies. NASA's is in Johnson Space Center, Houston, Texas.

Space agencies are always keen to gather more information on the effects of long-endurance spaceflight on the human body for future missions. Regular *ISS* stays last six months, although they can be upped to a year. As well as science, *ISS* astronauts have to service, fix, and mend equipment in the station or outside by spacewalks. Broken computers, air and coolant leaks, damaged solar arrays, faulty electronics, and worn-out machinery are just some of the regular headaches.

Soyuz TMA is the regular crew ferry.

Extravehicular Mobility Unit (EMU)

Many spare parts are stored in external compartments and must be accessed by spacewalking. A Japanese astronaut carries out maintenance (left), and a tethered Russian astronaut removes a Strela-2 cargo boom (right).

Strela-2 cargo boom

Orlan spacesuit

Canadarm 2 can grapple supply vessels to guide them in for docking, and even maneuver astronauts.

"ISS *is a vital resource to teach us how to live long-term in space.*" Michael Suffredini, *ISS* manager

Astronauts operate Canadarm 2 from the Robotic Work Station in Destiny. This station has two control joysticks and three screens. A second station is installed in the Cupola.

STATION DUTIES

ISS astronauts handle cargo deliveries from a variety of automated craft. Food, water, oxygen, clothes, laboratory equipment, satellites, and even creatures are unpacked carefully over weeks while the delivery ship stays docked.

A regular task is to unload the ferry craft and stow supplies around the station's modules.

The *ISS* has several laboratories. Columbus hosts experiments in fluid science (fluids that normally do not mix often do in microgravity), and how humans and other animals cope with spaceflight. Destiny houses a –112 °F (–26 °C) laboratory freezer for dangerous chemicals and an Earth imaging camera. JEM has experiment racks for studying crystals—which form with amazing purity in space—and a furnace to study combustion. JEM's outside platform is used for particle astronomy. Poisk includes a small medical center and Rassvet has an airlock to place experiments into the vacuum of space.

Astronaut Michael Foale performed experiments with living yeast microbes on a live video feed to Earth.

The Microgravity Science Glovebox in Destiny is where liquids, fire, and hazardous chemicals are tested.

Expedition 36 Flight Engineer Karen Nyberg tested two experimental satellites in microgravity—which is very difficult on Earth.

> *ISS* may **REACH** its **intended crew** of **SEVEN** when **new COMMERCIAL** crew **vehicles** become **AVAILABLE**.

LIFE IN SPACE

This zucchini plant grown by a crew member on the ISS floated freely in Destiny.

Old-timers say it takes three weeks to adjust to a space station's environment. Later comes the "three-month wall"—the peak of feeling isolated from loved ones on Earth.

LIVING IN FREEFALL

A space station in orbit whizzes along at an average speed of 17,000 miles (27,359 km) per hour, causing astronauts and any loose objects to float in microgravity as they constantly go forward yet "fall" toward the center of Earth.

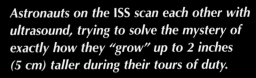

Hygiene's constant challenge: water forms drifting globules.

Years of spaceflight show that humans must complete two hours of strenuous exercise each day—here on Mir. *This maintains their fitness and strength, ahead of their return to Earth.*

Microgravity is a peculiar situation. There is no up or down. Astronauts can drift around. Heavy machinery is moved with the push of a finger. But long-term, microgravity has serious effects on the human body. Bones lose up to 1/60th of their structure each month. Muscle strength decays, especially in the legs. Astronauts' blood thins and their balance systems get disorientated.

Astronauts VALERI POLYAKOV holds the RECORD for the LONGEST continual time in SPACE at 437 DAYS 18 HOURS.

Astronauts on the ISS *scan each other with ultrasound, trying to solve the mystery of exactly how they "grow" up to 2 inches (5 cm) taller during their tours of duty.*

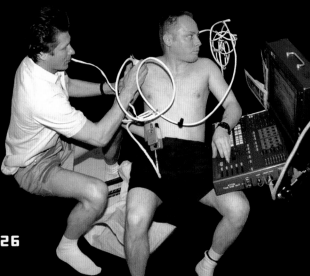

ISS *crew members Peggy Whitson and Valery Korzun shared a meal of floating hamburger and tomatoes in Zvezda. Both astronauts show a characteristic "puffy" face from upper-body fluid collection.*

"Saturday is housekeeping day on the ISS. Vacuuming filters, disinfecting surfaces..."

NASA astronaut Karen Nyberg

On the ISS, astronauts sleep overnight in a low-nitrogen chamber before donning their spacesuits.

A DIFFERENT EXISTENCE

When astronauts close their eyes to sleep, they see streaks of light from cosmic charged particles—space radiation. The constantly whirring air circulation removes all odors, which dulls the flavors of foods, so spicy sauces are added to many meals. On work days, every minute is pre-scheduled with activity—much of it highly technical. Regular sleep is hard to manage with eight sunrises and sunsets in each 24-hour day.

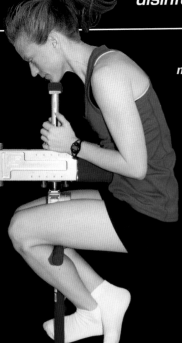

The Space Linear Acceleration Mass Measurement Device measures "weight," really mass, in microgravity.

Living in a space station space is hard work—but the persona rewards are immense. Many astronauts report intensely deep and spiritual feelings

FUTURE SPACE STATIONS

B eyond the *ISS*, NASA is looking at human interplanetary travel. Future Low Earth Orbit space stations are being planned by Russia (OPSEK) and by commercial companies keen to offer wealthy customers a space vacation.

International crew ship

Solar arrays

The Exploration Gateway Platform will be positioned at a Lagrange point, where the gravities of Earth, Moon, and Sun are balanced, needing little fuel to maintain. Its core is based on Node 4, an unused ISS unit.

NASA Reusable lunar lander

Solar arrays

EXPLORATION GATEWAY PLATFORM

1. **INTERNATIONAL MODULE** Based on Zvezda module from *ISS*, contains life support
2. **CONNECTING NODE** Central linking module
3. **HABITATION UNIT** Based on *ISS* MPLM
4. **UTILITY MODULE** Maneuvering system and airlock
5. **ORION SPACECRAFT** Command/service module

WAY STATIONS

Russia's planned Orbital Piloted Assembly and Experiment Complex (OPSEK) is based around its Nauka *ISS* module. The station will probably be made of four modules and used to assemble craft in orbit, for manned missions to the Moon, Mars, and possibly Saturn.

NASA-Boeing's Exploration Gateway Platform uses a cluster of *ISS*-derived modules towed into orbit between Earth and the Moon. It could be a base to launch Moon missions with reusable landers, and a testbed to develop ultra-reliable systems for manned Mars missions.

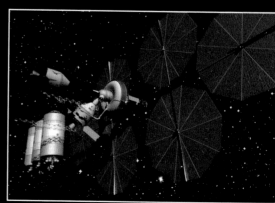

This NASA concept is for a propellant "gas station" supplied with liquid oxygen oxidizer made from lunar soil.

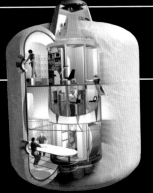

Transhab was an inflatable space habitat developed by NASA in the 1990s, then dropped.

> "I want to be part of something that is exciting, fun, and opens up great potential for our species."
>
> Robert Bigelow

SPACE HOTEL

Inflatable modules are flown into space folded up, then expanded in orbit. US hotel owner and space visionary Robert Bigelow hopes to entice tourists to a unique destination and support the USA's private spacecraft industry. *BEAM*—Bigelow Expandable Activity Module—is a small inflatable habitat derived from NASA's 1990s *Transhab*. A full-size version could yield three times the crew space of the *ISS*'s *Destiny* and offer better shielding from radiation and micrometeoroids. Bigelow's first space station, *Space Complex Bravo*, may follow.

The ISS will be funded by NASA until at least 2024, possibly 2028. Then it will be "deorbited" to face a fiery end in the atmosphere. There are currently no international plans to replace it.

Boeing CST-100 ferry ship

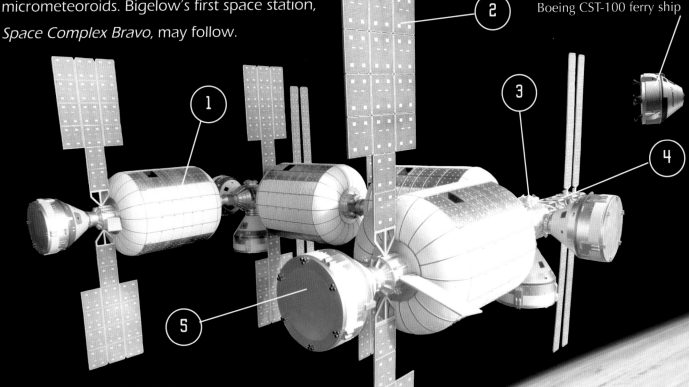

SPACE COMPLEX BRAVO

1. **BA 330** Expandable space habitation module
2. **SOLAR ARRAYS**
3. **CONNECTING NODE** Links modules and docking spacecraft
4. **PROPULSION BUS** Boosts and maintains orbital trajectory
5. **DOCKED CREW VEHICLE** Commercially available spacecraft of the time

> **60** days' **RENT** on **one-third** of a **BA 330** would be **$25 million** PLUS **$26.5 million** for a **RETURN seat** on a **COMMERCIAL** spaceship.

TECH FILES: SPACE STATIONS

SALYUT 1

MODULES One plus one docking port
CREW 3 occupied for 24 days
ORBITS Max altitude 134 miles (222 km); orbital period 88.5 minutes
LIFESPAN April 19, 1971 – October 11, 1971
FERRY CRAFT Soyuz 7K-OKS
MISSION Station systems test flight, microgravity experiments

SKYLAB

MODULES One plus Apollo Telescope Mount and docking adapter
CREW 3 (9 overall) occupied for 171 days
ORBITS Max altitude 274 miles (442 km); orbital period 93.4 minutes
LIFESPAN May 14, 1973 – July 11, 1979
FERRY CRAFT Apollo Command/Service Module
MISSION Sun/Earth observatory

SALYUT 3

MODULES One plus one docking port and armed with a Rikhter R-23 aircraft autocannon
CREW 2 occupied for 15 days
ORBITS Max altitude 170 miles (273 km); orbital period 89.1 minutes
LIFESPAN June 25, 1974 – January 24, 1975
FERRY CRAFT Soyuz 7K-T/A9
MISSION Secret Almaz military space station: Earth imaging

SALYUT 4

MODULES One plus one docking port
CREW 2 (4 overall) occupied for 92 days
ORBITS Max altitude 168 miles (270 km); orbital period 89.1 minutes
LIFESPAN December 26, 1974 – February 3, 1977
FERRY CRAFT Soyuz 7K-T
MISSION Solar and X-ray (deep space) telescopes, human spaceflight endurance testing

SALYUT 5

MODULES One plus one docking port
CREW 2 (4 overall) occupied for 67 days
ORBITS Max altitude 167 miles (269 km); orbital period 89 minutes
LIFESPAN June 22, 1976 – August 8, 1977
FERRY CRAFT Soyuz 7K-OKS
MISSION Secret Almaz military space station: Earth-observation imaging, studying aquarium fish in microgravity, solar observation

SALYUT 6

MODULES One plus two docking ports and a multispectral telescope
CREW 3 (32 overall) occupied 683 days
ORBITS Max altitude 171 miles (275 km); orbital period 89.1 minutes
LIFESPAN September 29, 1977 – July 29, 1982
FERRY/SUPPLY CRAFT Kosmos 1267 (unmanned TKS spacecraft), Soyuz 7K-T, Soyuz-T, Progress (unmanned Soyuz spacecraft)
MISSION Space observatory, Earth observatory with multispectral camera, radio observatory

SALYUT 7

MODULES One (same layout as Salyut 6)
CREW 3 (30 overall) occupied 816 days
ORBITS Max altitude 173 miles (278 km); orbital period 88.5 minutes
LIFESPAN April 19, 1971 – October 11, 1971
FERRY/SUPPLY CRAFT Kosmos 1443, Kosmos 1686, Soyuz-T, Progress
MISSION Science experiments human spaceflight endurance, EVAs

MIR

MODULES Six plus two docking ports, one extended by docking module
CREW 3 (visited by 39 manned missions in total) occupied 4592 days
ORBITS Max altitude 232 miles (374 km); orbital period 91.9 minutes
LIFESPAN February 20, 1986 / April 23, 1996 (last main module) – March 23, 2001
FERRY/SUPPLY CRAFT Soyuz-TM, Progress-M, Space Shuttle Orbiter
MISSION Continual human occupation in space, various experiments, growing crops in space, diplomatic relations

INTERNATIONAL SPACE STATION

MODULES 11 plus four docking ports and two EVA airlocks; total mass approximately 495 tons (450 tonnes)
CREW 6 (approximately 3–4 expeditions per year including many visiting crew)
ORBITS Max altitude 264 miles (425 km); orbital period 92.9 minutes
PROPOSED LIFESPAN 1998 – 2020
FERRY/SUPPLY/TRANSPORT CRAFT Soyuz-TM, Progress-M, Space Shuttle Orbiter, HTV, ATV, SpaceX Dragon, Orbital Sciences Cygnus
MISSION To study long-term effects of microgravity on humans for future interplanetary missions; growing crystals and plants; experiments with fluids and semiconductors in microgravity; testing wireless satellite technology in microgravity; studying animals in microgravity; many other experiments

GLOSSARY

ATMOSPHERE layer of gases around a space object such as a planet

ATTITUDE position of a spacecraft, for example, its angle in relation to Earth, or pointing at a star

DEORBIT make a spacecraft leave its regular orbit, either flying away into deep space, or returning down to its planet or moon—perhaps burning up on reentry

DOCK in space, when two craft or modules join together, especially so that astronauts, equipment, and other objects can pass between them, usually through a linking tunnel

EVA Extra Vehicular Activity, being outside a craft in space, often called a spacewalk

FERRY CRAFT in space, a craft that regularly takes goods and supplies up to a space station, and/or returns objects—often including waste—back to Earth or burn-up during reentry

GRAVITY force of attraction between objects, which is especially huge for massive objects like planets and stars

MASS amount of matter in an object, in the form of numbers and kinds of atoms

MICROGRAVITY where the force of gravity from a nearby object, like a planet, is extremely weak or almost zero

MODULE section, part or unit of a larger structure

ORBIT regular path of one object around a larger one, determined by the speed, mass and gravity of the objects

REENTRY returning from space to an object such as a planet, when friction with the thickening atmosphere slows the spacecraft but also causes immense heat

RPM revolutions per minute

SATELLITE space object that goes around or orbits another, including natural satellites like the Moon orbiting Earth or Earth orbiting the Sun, and man-made satellites—including space stations

SOLAR ARRAY large panel or area of solar cells that turn the energy of sunlight into electrical power

TRUSS long, girder-like structure with many repeating units, usually square or triangular in shape, that forms part of a larger rigid framework

INDEX